The CONCRETE RIVER

poems by

Luis J. Rodríguez

CURBSTONE PRESS

"The Best of Us" and "First Day of Work" were performed in the poetry theater production "Metaphoria: Chicago Poetry Theater With a Twist" for three nights in October, 1989 at the Firehouse Theater in Chicago.

"Waiting," "Jarocho Blues," and "Lips" were performed in December, 1989 as part of the poetry performance piece "Concrete Conversations: Poetry From Both Sides Of the Street," at Club Lower Links, Chicago.

Some of the poems have appeared in *201: The Homenaje a la Ciudad de Los Angeles Anthology; Bulletin for the Center for Puerto Rican Studies; Catechumenate; Chicano Poetry of the First Annual Chicano Poetry Festival; Chicago Saloon Poets;* MARCH/Abrazo Press; *Chiron Review; Dial-a-Poem Chicago; Dynamics of Violence; Electrum; Hammers; Hispanic Link; Howling Dog; Lies Of Our Time; Literati Chicago; The Los Angeles Times; Milestones Magazine; Mother Tongues;* N magazine; *Obras; ONTHEBUS; The People's Tribune; Poetry East; Poetry U.S.A.; Tonantzin; Touchstone; The Unifier;* and *With The Wind At My Back And Ink In My Blood,* an anthology of poems by the homeless.

Front cover photograph by Chuck Kramer

Cover design by Stone Graphics
Printed in the U.S. on acid-free paper

ISBN: 0-915306-42-5
Library of Congress number: 90-56217

This publication was supported in part by donations, and by grants from The National Endowment for the Arts, and the Connecticut Commission on the Arts, a state agency whose funds are recommended by the Governor and appropriated by the State Legislature.

CURBSTONE PRESS
321 Jackson Street
Willimantic, CT 06226

for
NELSON PEERY

who taught me the poetry of the fight,
and the fight in the poetry.

"It takes a hell of a miracle for some god to create a madman."
—overheard at Wendy's Restaurant in Chicago, 1986

CONTENTS

IV. MUSIC OF THE MILL

V. A HARVEST OF EYES

THE CONCRETE RIVER

PRELUDE TO A HEARTBEAT

WATTS BLEEDS

Watts bleeds
leaving stained reminders
on dusty sidewalks.

Here where I strut alone
as glass lies broken by my feet
and a blanket of darkness is slung
across the wooden shacks
of *nuestra colonia.*

Watts bleeds
dripping from carcasses of dreams:
Where despair
is old people
sitting on torn patio sofas
with empty eyes
and children running down alleys
with big sticks.

Watts bleeds
on vacant lots
and burned-out buildings—
temples desolated by a people's rage.

Where fear is a deep river.
Where hate is an overgrown weed.

Watts bleeds
even as we laugh,
recall good times,
drink and welcome daylight
through the broken windshield
of an old Impala.

Here is Watts of my youth,
where teachers threw me
from classroom to classroom,
not knowing where I could fit in.

Where I learned to fight or run,
where I zigzagged down alleys,
jumped over fences,
and raced by graffiti on crumbling
factory walls.

Where we played
between the boxcars,
bleeding from
broken limbs and torn flesh,
and where years later
we shot up *carga*
in the playground
of our childhood.

Watts bleeds
as the shadow of the damned
engulfs all the *chinga* of our lives.

In the warmth of a summer night,
gunshots echo their deadly song
through the silence of fear;
prelude to a heartbeat.

Watts bleeds
as I bled
getting laid-off from work,
standing by my baby's crib,
touching his soft cheek
and fingering his small hand

as dreams shatter again,
dreams of fathers
for little men.

Watts bleeds
and the city hemorrhages,
unable to stop the flow
from this swollen and festering sore.

Oh bloom, you trampled flower!
Come alive as once
you tried to do from the ashes.

Watts, bleeding and angry,
you will be free.

THE COLDEST DAY

Shadows moved chairs and plates
from tables, whispering,
because that's what people do
in the dark.

To me, it was the coldest day in the world,
there in sunny LA,
the day the gas and the lights
were shut off because bills
went unpaid.

Candles lit the corner of rooms
and fired-up bricks glowed with warmth
but the iciness broke through
the splintered walls.

I took a bath in frigid waters.
I wanted to jump out and run away,
but Mama kept sticking me in,
rubbing me hard with soap
and saying a shiver of words
to comfort me:
This is the only way, she'd say,
the only way...

It was the coldest day in the world.
It could not be the only way!
That night we drove around for blocks
to find a place to eat.
We stopped in front of a restaurant.
I looked at the window
and refused to enter.

"What's the matter?" Mama demanded.

I pointed to a sign on the restaurant door.
It read: "Come In, Cold Inside."

DEATHWATCH

1.
There is a room in the old house
where the dead sleep,
not dead like without life,
dead like winter,
breathing the moments in
but decay everywhere.

In spring, blossoms burn with color
but each wrinkle, every new invasion
of gray over black on your head
is only a fraction step
in your lifelong demise.

Living with you, Pop,
was like being on a deathwatch.
A slow dying of day, a candle flickering.
What of the man who taught high school
in *Ciudad Juárez,* wrote biology books
and stormed the rigid government-
controlled system there—
the one who dared new life?

Where have you been, my father?
You were always escaping,
always a faint memory of fire,
a rumor of ardor;
sentenced to leaving
but never gone.

2.
He will never understand
the silence that drove me to the alley,

that kept me tied
to the gravel of deadly play;
why I wanted to die, just to know him.

One day I got drunk with a work crew
and everyone talked about their
imprisoned dads, their junkie dads, their no-dads
and I said I had a dad, but I never heard him
say love, never heard him say son,
and how I wished he wasn't my dad,
but the others yelled back:
How can you judge?
How do you know what he had to do
to be there! Could I do better?
Could I walk in his shoes
and pretend a presence?

3.
He wasn't always there.
Lisa died as an infant
after accidently eating *chicharrones*
he sold on cobblestone streets in Mexico.
Seni was abandoned and left with his mom.
A story tells of a young Seni who answered the door
to a stranger, wet from a storm.
She called out, "Mama Piri"—
she always called her grandmother mama—
who rushed into the room and told her,
"Don't worry...it's only your father."

Alberto and Mario, born of different women,
one of whom died giving birth,
stayed in Mexico when Dad left.
By then he had married Mama. She was 11 years younger
and he was almost 40 and still running.
Three more children were born across the border

to become U.S. citizens.
Then a long drive to Watts
where another daughter came.
These were the children he came home to,
the ones who did not get away.
How can I judge?

4.
An Indian-shawled woman trekked across
mountains and desert on an old burro,
just outside the village of Coahuayutla.
In her arms was a baby in weavings,
whimpering in spurts, as the heat
bore down harder with each step
and snakes dangled close to them
from gnarled trees.

Bandits emerged from out of the cactus groves.
"Give us your money, if your life has any value."
The woman pleaded mercy, saying her husband
was with Pancho Villa
and she had to leave because *federales*
were going to raid her town.
"We don't care about no revolution,"
a bandit said. "Nobody cares for us,
but us...give us what you got."
She held close the tied wrappings filled with infant.
Another bandit saw the baby and said:
"This is your child, mother?"
"And of a revolutionary," she replied.
"Then go...your mother-love
has won you a life."
My grandmother continued on her way;
Dad had crossed his first *frontera*.

5.
Trust was a tree that never stayed rooted;
never to trust a hope of family
never to nurture the branches of a child
awake with ripening fruit.
He trusted less the love we gave
as he mistrusted doctors.
He seldom went to doctors.

One time doctors put him in a hospital
for tests. He had a cough that wouldn't
go away. They had him splayed and tied with tubes
to monitors and plastic bottles.
After a few days, he called my brother and me
to take his car and wait in front of the hospital
steps. When we got there my dad
ran from the front door and into the car.
He had removed all the attachments,
put on his clothes,
sneaked past the nurses station,
and waited by a phone booth for our arrival.
He claimed the hospital was holding
him hostage for the insurance money.
Doctors called and demanded
his return. Dad said never.
He had his own remedies.

6.
He was the one who braved the world's
most heavily-guarded border,
the one who sold pots, pans, and insurance,
and worked construction sites,
the one who endured
the degradations of school administrators,
who refused his credentials,
forced to be a janitor—

what they called a "laboratory technician"—
cleaning up animal cages and classrooms;
the closest he would get to a profession.

Every so often, Dad hauled home
hamsters, tarantulas, king snakes,
and fossiled rocks.
My father, the "biologist," named
all the trees and plants
in our yard, gave them stickers
with unpronounceable syllables.
He even renamed us:
I was *Grillo*—cricket;
my brother became *Rano,* the frog;
Ana was *La Pata,* the duck;
And Gloria, he transformed into *La Cucaracha:*
Cockroach.
By renaming things, he reclaimed them.

7.
All around the room are mounds of papers:
Junk mail, coupons, envelopes (unopened & empty),
much of this sticking out of drawers,
on floor piles—in a shapeless heap
in the corner. On the wooden end
of a bed is a ball made up of thousands
of rubber bands. Cereal boxes
are thrown about everywhere,
some half full. There are writing
tablets piled on one side, filled
with numbers, numbers without pattern,
that you write over and over:
obsessed.

For years your silence
was greeting and departure,
a vocal disengagement.
I see you now walking around in rags,
your eyes glued to Spanish-language *novelas,*
keen to every nuance of voice and movement,

what you rarely gave to me.
This silence is now comfort.

We almost made it, eh Pop?
From the times when you came home late
and gathered up children in both arms
as wide as a gentle wind
to this old guy, visited by police and social workers,
talking to air, accused of lunacy.
I never knew you.
Losing you was all there was.

TIA CHUCHA

Every few years
Tía Chucha would visit the family
in a tornado of song
and open us up
as if we were an overripe avocado.
She was a dumpy, black-haired
creature of upheaval,
who often came unannounced
with a bag of presents
including home-made perfumes and colognes
that smelled something like
rotting fish
on a hot day at the tuna cannery.

They said she was crazy.
Oh sure, she once ran out naked
to catch the postman
with a letter that didn't belong to us.
I mean, she had this annoying habit
of boarding city buses
and singing at the top of her voice
(one bus driver even refused to go on
until she got off).
But crazy?

To me, she was the wisp
of the wind's freedom,
a music-maker
who once tried to teach me guitar
but ended up singing
and singing,
me listening,
and her singing

until I put the instrument down
and watched the clock
click the lesson time away.

I didn't learn guitar,
but I learned something
about her craving
for the new, the unbroken
...so she could break it.
Periodically she banished
herself from the family
and was the better for it.

I secretly admired Tía Chucha.
She was always quick with a story,
another *"Pepito"* joke,
or a hand-written lyric
that she would produce
regardless of the occasion.

She was a despot
of desire;
uncontainable
as a splash of water
on a varnished table.

I wanted to remove
the layers
of unnatural seeing
the way Tía Chucha beheld
the world, with first eyes,
like an infant
who can discern
the elixir
within milk.

I wanted to be
one of the prizes
she stuffed into
her rumpled bag.

SPEAKING WITH HANDS

There were no markets in Watts.
There were these small corner stores
we called *marketas*
who charged more money
for cheaper goods than what existed
in other parts of town.
The owners were often thieves in white coats
who talked to you like animals,
who knew you had no options;
who knew Watts was the preferred landfill
of the city.

One time, Mama started an argument
at the cash register.
In her broken English,
speaking with her hands,
she had us children stand around her
as she fought with the grocer
on prices & quality & dignity.

Mama became a woman swept
by a sobering madness;
she must have been what Moses saw
in the burning bush,
a pillar of fire,
consuming the still air
that reeked of overripe fruit
and bad meat from the frozen food
section.

She refused to leave
until the owner called the police.
The police came and argued too,
but Mama wouldn't stop.
They pulled her into the parking lot,
called her crazy...
and then Mama showed them crazy!

They didn't know what to do
but let her go, and Mama took us children
back toward home, tired of being tired.

NIGHT DANCING: WATTS 1975-78

Nothing in Watts whispers.
Every open window is a shout,
a night dance to a driving
pulse that crashes through
the broken walls of a
Jordan Downs second-floor flat.

Conga sounds and synthesizers
compete against the drunken
laughter and angry talk
of young crips whose world
is bigger than this place
but never as important.

Here innocence and terror
are woven into the summer
breeze as the cries of the
'hood' deliver sacrifices
of sound and flesh,
as a mother's milk flows,

and the heat hangs on you
like a wet blanket.
All begins to blend, come apart;
all is loving, destroying,
while homegirls dance a jig
to a repertoire of police sirens.

SOUNDTRACKS

Sometimes terror comes
in the song of birds,
in the slight things.
Sometimes it comes
in whispers of night,
in the quiet, delicate moments
before the implosions of passion,
hate and fear rise to the surface,
fiery and bright.

       Through the greenery of shrubs,
telephone poles,
the hum of powerlines,
come a symphony of crickets
or the coos of a dove,
seeming to follow our little disasters.
A kind of soundtrack for fear.
Many times I hear these sounds
and, from the mouth of memory,
I emerge, a small boy,

back to a time when an eviction
forced the family to move in
with my oldest sister—
eleven of us crammed into a small apartment.
The children slept on makeshift bedding
thrown about the living room floor.
Most of our belongings
stuffed into a garage.

There were yells, cries—
demands on my dad,

who was often out of work,
or claims by my sister
that her husband had another woman.
The boys fought with the girls,
who, in turn, tore into scraggly dolls.
I sought refuge in the street.

One night, I came home late,
after having stocked up on
licorice and bubblegum
and walked past police cars
and an ambulance.
Colored lights whirled
across the tense faces of neighbors
who stood on patches
of grass and driveway.
I pushed through low voices
and entered the house: blood
splattered on a far wall.

Moments before, my sister
had been brushing her daughter's hair
when, who knows why,
she pulled at the long strands.
The girl's screams
brought in my sister's husband.
An argument ensued. Vicious words.
Accusations.

My sister plucked a fingernail file
from the bathroom sink.
It glistened in front
of my brother-in-law's face.
He grabbed for her hand. The nail file
plunged into his arm. Mom and Dad rushed in,
ramming my sister against the wall;

nail file crashed steely bright
onto the peeling linoleum floor.

When I got there,
excited tones
retold what happened.
Then I heard it, a sound,
far off, like an easy thunder,
a crazy dove's cooing.

Sometimes police cars screeched
around corners, and children
rushed out of doors
as home fires
extinguished in violence.

Then the soft sounds of the season
played like a deadly score
that you'd remember
every time the leaves
played them back.

DANCING ON A GRAVE

DANCING ON A GRAVE

Old Man Lopez—
with 14 children
from four wives—
wanted to be buried
with *Sinaloenses*
dancing on his grave
to the tune of
"La Ultima Paranda"
and Mexican beer
poured over the casket
in the sign of the cross.

THE VILLAGE

Aliso Village. East LA.
Welfare/unemployment/teenposts.
Brown/black villagers
wade in a sea of stucco green

imitating cool, as 14-year-old
girls, with babies by their feet,
sing oldies from darkened porches,
here, across the LA River,

concrete border
of scrawled walls,
railroad tracks, and sweatshops,
here, where we remade revolution

in our images. Here,
where at 18 years old and dying,
I asked her to marry me.

I carry the village in tattoos
across my arms.

CHOTA

Here I lie, embraced by the miasmic draft
of side-street America;
a voice cuts into the still air.
A police officer stands above me
and the gum stains on Seventh Street.

Chota.

Soon I sit battered, humiliated,
in the dankness of a jail cell;
officers wallow around
contemplating my "suicide."

But this time
they will have to kill me.
Each time a fist smashes
across my belly, pummels my face,
I reach out
to the cries of the curb,
the ballads out of broken brick,
and the smoky outline of a woman's face
burned onto a cell wall.

They will have to kill me!

WRITHING SKELETONS

I welcome writhing skeletons
to my door—partners
of past burnings.

They come to see me off
as downtown's peeping-tom eyes
intrude into my Fourth Street flat.

Each going a painful
erasing of myself.

They come to tear me away
as Hollenbeck Park smiles
and laughing children rush by
on wings of canvas and suede.

THE CONCRETE RIVER

We sink into the dust,
Baba and me,
Beneath brush of prickly leaves;
Ivy strangling trees—singing
Our last rites of *locura*.
Homeboys. Worshipping God-fumes
Out of spray cans.

Our backs press up against
A corrugated steel fence
Along the dried banks
Of a concrete river.
Spray-painted outpourings
On walls offer a chaos
Of color for the eyes.

Home for now. Hidden in weeds.
Furnished with stained mattresses
And plastic milk crates.
Wood planks thrust into
             thick branches
             serves as roof.
The door is a torn cloth curtain
             (knock before entering).
Home for now, sandwiched
In between the maddening days.

We aim spray into paper bags.
Suckle them. Take deep breaths.
An echo of steel-sounds grates the sky.
Home for now. Along an urban-spawned
Stream of muck, we gargle in
The technicolor synthesized madness.

This river, this concrete river,
Becomes a steaming, bubbling
Snake of water, pouring over
Nightmares of wakefulness;
Pouring out a rush of birds;
A flow of clear liquid
On a cloudless day.
Not like the black oil stains we lie in,
Not like the factory air engulfing us;
Not this plastic death in a can.

Sun rays dance on the surface.
Gray fish fidget below the sheen.
And us looking like Huckleberry Finns/
Tom Sawyers, with stick fishing poles,
As dew drips off low branches
As if it were earth's breast milk.

Oh, we should be novas of our born days.
We should be scraping wet dirt
                    with calloused toes.
We should be flowering petals
                    playing ball.

Soon water/fish/dew wane into
A pulsating whiteness.
I enter a tunnel of circles,
Swimming to a glare of lights.
Family and friends beckon me.
I want to be there,
In perpetual dreaming;
In the din of exquisite screams.
I want to know this mother-comfort
Surging through me.

I am a sliver of blazing ember
                 entering a womb of brightness.
I am a hovering spectre shedding
                 scarred flesh.
I am a clown sneaking out of a painted
                 mouth in the sky.
I am your son, *amá,* seeking
                 the security of shadows,
                 fleeing weary eyes
                 bursting brown behind
                 a sewing machine.
I am your brother, the one you
                 threw off rooftops, tore into
                 with rage—the one you visited,
                 a rag of a boy, lying
                 in a hospital bed, ruptured.
I am friend of books, prey of cops,
                 lover of the *barrio* women
                 selling hamburgers and tacos
                 at the P&G Burger Stand.

I welcome this heavy shroud.
I want to be buried in it—
To be sculptured marble
In craftier hands.

Soon an electrified hum sinks teeth
Into brain—then claws
Surround me, pull at me,
Back to the dust, to the concrete river.

Let me go!—to stay entangled
In this mesh of barbed serenity!
But over me is a face,
Mouth breathing back life.

I feel the gush of air,
The pebbles and debris beneath me.

"Give me the bag, man," I slur.
"No way! You died, man," Baba said.
"You stopped breathing and died."
"I have to go back!...you don't
            understand..."

I try to get up, to reach the sky.
Oh, for the lights—for this whore
            of a Sun,
To blind me. To entice me to burn.
Come back! Let me swing in delight
To the haunting knell,
To pierce colors of virgin skies.
Not here, along a concrete river,
But there—licked by tongues of flame!

THE BEST OF US

(to Marcia Gonzales, whose voice is captured here,
and to the memory of Miguel Robles)

Epitaphs hang like clothes on a line.
They are smeared with a whitewash,
the color of injustice.
Hypocritical prayers fill the sweat of days,
flowing down the empty lots and alleys
where my boy plays.
Denial clings to my skin;
a breathy wind keeps bringing it back.
They say I should be glad I do not hunger,
but I'm starving with the pangs of discontent.
The nightmares never cease:
A shackled corpse on blood-soaked sheets.
The .357 magnum's smoking nostril at my belly.
A shadowed face screaming for reprisals.
A child with unknowing eyes asking for his father.

Birdlike, I hover above the grave,
quivering on broken wings.
Inside is a statue of clay,
your body,
made-over with a mouth clenched in silence.
I wait for the moment when you rise.
I want to pour over you this aborted love,
draining from me along with tears.
You never do awaken.
You never provide a hint of recognition.
They say it's God's will. They say I must go on.
I do—carrying you with me.
But every path stops with you.
Every beginning is you.
If not for this seed growing to manhood,

a seed you never see change into its seasons,
I would fail to meet every dawn.
Even now I try to disembark.
But everything—
the wind on my face,
the sparkle of stars at night,
the blast of sun on my back—
is as it was when you tenderly fashioned
my body beneath you.

*"Ladies and gentlemen of the jury: The prosecution will show
how the plaintiff in this case gave birth to a son, who is the
true child of the deceased. And how his untimely death has
deprived this infant boy of ever knowing his father, or the
love, care, and attention that he could have provided, if..."*

Transcript machines clicking.
Witnesses, looking like sad paintings,
sit in pews of swirled wood.
Policemen laugh in the hallways.
For months I visit these marbled corridors,
push myself through sterilized aisles
and think of facing the jury,
of tearing my eyes out of their sockets,
and saying: "Take these—see what I have seen!"
The lies come dressed in suits and ties;
they lurk behind badges and smothered grins.
Take these eyes and know the truth.
Instead, I'm drowning in a sea of legal terms,
forensic jargon—policies and procedures.
More lies.

When it's my turn to testify, I stutter.
It's a voice of lessened humanity.

A woman's bitter musings
through a veil of solitude.
A plea crawling from the curbside.
They have my name and thereby possess me.
I am that *chola*,
that street-girl buried in the crazy life.
I did not commit any crime.
But I am a woman of dark skin
and a darker heritage.
This is my crime.

"Will you tell the truth, the whole truth, and nothing but the
truth, so help you God?
"I will."
"State your name and address for the record please."
"My name is Delia Torres...but everyone calls me Dee Dee. I
live on 1132 Hazard Avenue, East Los Angeles."
"Okay, Delia—Dee Dee—will you please tell the jury what
happened the night of March 15, 1981...and please be as
explicit as you can. You understand explicit, don't you?"
"Yes sir, I mean, I know what you mean...sir—"
"'Yes' is a good enough answer, thank you. Now tell us, in
your own words, what happened?"

What I couldn't tell:
The way the night seemed to sing into being
on a day full of the lust of spring.
The way your mom carefully emptied
a pot of water that had been soaking with beans.
How your brother Tony sat in front of the TV,
its greenish-blue lights changing tints
across his face.
This was my first dinner with your family.
Alone, pregnant, I finally felt enveloped

in firm arms.
A former ward of the state, abandoned,
I had to scrape a life out of narrow streets...
until your family took me in.
They made me believe there could be something
like home, like love,
something I could wake up to and touch—
that it was not an illusion.
Your mother made a funny remark
and something alien—laughter—burst forth
from me,
like a butterfly out of a cocoon
woven from warmth inside.
And everyone, including your dad,
lying in bed then
with a broken thigh bone from a work injury,
accepted me,
made me want to be your wife,
the mother of your child.
Remember how you smiled that day...
how you and your brother
playfully pushed each other and I said,
"Don't make me come in and belt you guys."

*"Walter Joseph Coles, 14 years as an officer of the Los
Angeles County Sheriff's Department. Numerous citations
for brave conduct. A father of three boys. On March 15,
1981, Deputy Coles shot and killed one, Guillermo
"Memo" Tovar, 17 years old, and injured one, Antonio
"Tony" Tovar, 19 years old. Said suspects were believed to
be endangering the life of Deputy Coles at the time of the
incident. The sheriff's office interdepartmental review finds
this to be a case of justifiable homicide due to
circumstances of possible injury or death to said officer.*

Following routine paid suspension, Deputy Coles has been reinstated and transferred to another subdivision of the county."

Oh, I want to scream out my lungs!
The things they say about you!
How you were once caught joyriding,
that you were a gang member.
A delinquent.
But that's not you!
You were Memo,
a handsome *prieto* with a face
that could have been carved
from the darkest mahogany.
Memo, with sharp brown eyes
that pierced the placid smiles
and phony demeanors the rest of us wore as masks.
You played football, baseball—ran track.
You planned to get good grades
and go to college...to be somebody decent.
Remember the time we walked home from school
and you spotted a tall hedge of ivy.
Remember. You tossed up a challenge.
"You think I can jump over it?"
The hedge was high and bushy.
I said no.
But you moved back, bent low
and took in the distance.
Then you got on your hands,
paused there on the sidewalk,
and suddenly leaped forward—running fast,
like an Olympic athlete,
like an Indian over rocky streams.
When you jumped, it was so smooth
you could have been a kite of bright colors,

sailing on a low wind,
and me holding the string.
You made it over. You always made it over.
Memo, you were the best of us.

"Mr. Coles, isn't it a fact that you've had a track record of
abuse, beatings, and uncontrolled violent tempers—"
"No, this is totally unfounded."
"Then why is there a record of numerous complaints of
unwarranted arrests and shootings in those communities,
black and Mexican, in which you have served in the capacity
of a peace officer in the County of Los Angeles?"
"Those are unsubstantiated claims."
"Now, Mr. Coles, they can't all be wrong."
"I object, your honor—"
"Objection sustained...Please continue another line of
questioning, counsel."
"Okay then, isn't it true, Mr. Coles, that the willful and
unlawful murder of this boy, and the maiming of his brother,
are acts that culminated a career-long pattern of brutality?"
"No, it's not. I stand on a record of exceptional conduct."

You can't know.
After the shootings,
you were taken to the prison ward
of the County Hospital.
They put leather straps on your arms and legs
but you couldn't move anyway.
They put tubes through your mouth
that couldn't speak anyway.
Your father and mother were also handcuffed,
even with the cast on your dad's leg.
You can't know how all your friends—
Danny Boy, Filo, Serafin—were arrested

and booked for your murder!
Because they happened to be there!
And your brother Tony, shot in the head,
but still alive. His ear gone.
You can't know how mangled your body looked;
bruised and caked with a kind of black paste
they said was your blood.

*"Ms. Torres, we know this is difficult for you...but please
try to compose yourself. Now, tell the court what you saw,
as you experienced it, that night of the shootings...Take
your time...Ms. Torres, Ms. Torres...Your honor, I think
she's fainted."*

I try and try to understand it.
To know where the night failed us.
But I can't. We did nothing wrong.
It started out as a beautiful day.
That afternoon Danny Boy, Filo, and Serafin
came over with a case of beer:
Talking the day away.
Then they drove by, slow,
in a black and white vehicle—
Deputy Coles and Deputy Daryl Tatum:
An Anglo cop and a black cop.
Coles got out of the car and started shouting.
I ran to the window and looked outside.
All of you were spread-eagled
with your hands across the car's hood.
"What's going on, Dee Dee?" your mother asked.
"I don't know. It's cops," I answered.
"They got Memo and the boys."
Then Tony got up.
"What? They got Memo!"

Before I knew it he ran out.
I looked out the window
and saw Tony run up to the officers.
There was arguing.
Danny Boy said something,
I don't know what, but I saw Coles
strike him in the belly with his flashlight.
You turned around and Tatum pushed you back.
Then for no reason at all,
Coles turned to Tony and started calling him
all kinds of names.
From then on everything seemed like a dream.
Tony ran. Coles dashed after him.
Tatum pulled out a gun and held it over you
and the other guys.
Tony rushed into the house but Coles
tackled him in the living room.
A lamp crashed to the floor.
Your mother screamed.
I could hear your dad shout from the bedroom,
"What's going on in there?"
I backed into the kitchen,
next to your mom—
instinctively placing a hand
over my womb.
Then Coles, standing over Tony,
who laid there on the floor,
got out his gun from a black leather holster.
And I heard your mother shout, "No, not *mijo,* no!"
But he fired it. He fired at Tony's head,
him laying there.
I screamed, and then you burst in.
You came in yelling as you jumped on Coles' back.
Coles fell forward.
Then he grappled with you.
Somehow he pushed you off

and you landed on the sofa.
But Coles didn't hesitate.
He had the gun ready, cocked.
It went off again in a flash of fire.
You fell back, holding your belly, groaning.
Your dad crawled into the living room
and saw you sink into the sofa.
Deputy Tatum ran into the house
just then and looked at everything:
the blood, the broken lamp, the bodies...
your fainted mother on the kitchen floor—
Deputy Coles with his gun pointed at me.
I stood silent, like I wasn't there,
frozen by a sound shrouded in terror.
Paralyzed, my arms don't move, my feet don't move,
my brain on hold, unable to talk;
only the beating of a heart continued.
Deputy Tatum dropped his arm
that had been holding a gun.
In a muffled tenor,
breaking the quiet that was beginning
to strangle me,
he said, "Oh my God, oh my God..."

"Will the foreman please step forward. Has the jury reached a verdict?
"Yes, we have, your honor."
"And what is that verdict, please?"
"We find the defendant, Walter J. Coles, not guilty as charged."

Do you know about boys, Mister Coles?
Do you know about what it takes
to see their faces

40

hide in the pain
of growing into men?

*"Miss Torres, we feel you must know the progress of your
son, Guillermo, Jr. He is very much into himself. Other kids
try to play with him, but he just sits in a corner, alone.
Now, he is a very intelligent boy, and extremely helpful for
a three-year-old. For example, Guillermo likes to pick up
chairs and toys after everyone is through for the day. But
he doesn't participate in the games we play as a group.
Now...we don't want to force him, but we feel you must
know about this situation so we can work together in
bringing him out. Miss Torres, can you please tell us what,
if anything, may be bothering him..."*

Everything began to crumble then.
Tony never did get over it;
the anger gnawing at him, day after day.
He's in jail now, but you know that.
Your father stopped working.
It was as if he stopped living too.
His lifelong belief in this country,
its promises, betrayed.
Why then did he sweat and labor all his life?
Why did he fight overseas,
carrying the American flag on a hill in Korea?
Your mom, bless her, keeps the house going,
cleaning everyday and seeing that the crumbling
won't cave in on her.
Oh we took the case to civil court, sure,
filing an unlawful death suit.
But the time passed on, our money went dry,
and there is only $4,000 in reparations.
I wish something would shatter my skull

and this memory. I'm wrong, I know,
but how does one be right about this?
Tell me, Memo?
How can I find the courage—
to stop waking up night after night,
to stop this crying into wilted flowers?
Our son keeps growing.
What answers do I give him?
How do I explain?
"Well, *mijito,* your daddy had his guts blown out
by a racist cop and $4,000 is supposed to make it better."

"We have come together here to demand justice. So many
of our sons have been killed. So many of our fathers...this
must stop now! The community has to pool its resources—
crossing barrio lines, language lines—and demand an end
to this armed camp called East Los Angeles. The police
have the power of life and death here. We must take this
power from them...Take our destiny into our hands, to forge
a community worthy of its residents; one which will benefit
all of us—documented or undocumented, young or old,
man or woman...Memo Tovar still lives—in our memory
and in our struggle..¡Ya Basta! No more police murders!"

We almost left the neighborhood.
We almost had to.
Cops harassed us every day,
watching us come and go.
But people rallied around us,
helping take care of your mom
and dad, the boy and me.
Others have been beaten,
killed.
So there have been protests, marches.
They are gathering again today,

and I will march with them.
They are organizing an anti-police abuse group,
and I will be at the meetings.
The community has stepped into your shoes—
to protect your interests now that you can't.
I have hope for our child—
and for all the children here and everywhere
whose mothers have known the sorrow
of withered breasts,
but also the joy of watching
these cords of humanity
blossom in the sun.

I got a job—finally!—
and your boy is in day care,
doing so much better!
Oh, smile for me, Memo,
smile and break apart
the crystal walls of your death
surrounding us.
Climb out of this hole,
trample the flowers,
be this dream,
this man.
My Memo...

THE THRESHOLD

I enter a door carved with knife slashes
across the grain and the names of homeboys
penned in colored marker or in spraypaint.
I stand there at the threshold
and scan the burning room with murals
on all the walls while the routine of night
continues toward its end.

In a corner is a woman in teased
hair, eyes encircled by dark wine mascara.
A sparkle pulsates from her gaze as stars
do at the edge of sky.
The woman leans against the mural
of a large snake with a syringe
in its scaly grasp.

She no longer has that girl's flesh.
She no longer smells of fresh grass
following a rain. She punctures a vein,
fills it with clear liquid and crumbles
into dust piles upon the bed.
Outside, a curled vine scrapes the window
as the lungs of dawn slowly breathe a morning
            to birth.

But inside, we dance in the terrain of the horse,
leavening into a bread of explosive desire.
I am sitting on the corner of the bed
next to blood drops on the blanket
as a needle falls to the floor, and she,
naked from the waist up, lies flat, smiling
through the thickness of a black hole that seems
            to engulf her face.

THE TWENTY-NINTH

(By 1970, about 22 percent of the Vietnam War casualties came from Spanish-speaking communities. Yet at that time this population made up less than six percent of the U.S. total. In protest, some 30,000 people from across the American Southwest marched through the heart of East Los Angeles.)

August 29, 1970—I emerged out of an old, bumpy bus on the Atlantic Boulevard line and entered a crowd snaking through the steaming streets and by the red-dirt yards of the city's east side. I hadn't been fully aware of my own sense of outrage until, melding with other marchers, I found myself raising a fist in the air. I was a street kid then: 16 years old, in gang attire and earring. I had no idea how significant the protest would be. Frankly, I had only come to party.

We continued past stretches of furniture stores, used car lots and cemeteries. Many store keepers closed early, pulling down rusty iron enclosures. Others, small vendors of wares and food, came out to provide drink—relief on that broiling day. Around me marched young mothers with babies in strollers, factory hands, *cholos*, uniformed Brown Berets (the Mexican version of the Black Panthers) in cadence, a newly-wed couple (still in tuxedo and wedding gown)—young and old alike.

We turned onto Whittier Boulevard, joined by people from the neighborhoods. Instances of battle flared up at alleys and side streets. Young dudes and cops clashed. But most of us kept up the stride. At Laguna Park, the multitude laid out on the grass. Children played. Beer got passed around. Voices burst out in song. Speeches, music, and street theater filled the air. I made my way to a nearby liquor store. The store had closed early. A number of us wanted to get more to drink. A shotgun, pushed against my head, caused me to jerk backward. "Move, or I'll blow your fuckin' head off," a sheriff's deputy ordered. I left, wandering through feet and bodies, coolers and blankets.

At the park's edge, a brown line of deputies—armed with high-powered rifles, billy clubs and tear gas launchers— began to swagger toward the crowd. Those who hesitated were mowed down by swinging clubs. A group of people held arms to stop the rioting police from getting to the families. I turned toward the throng of officers. One guy told me to go back, "We'll fight tomorrow." Then it hit me: There are no more tomorrows for me. I had enough at the hands of alien authority. So come then, you helmeted, marching wall of state power. Come and try to blacken this grass, this shirt of colors, this festive park filled with infants and mothers and old men, surging forth in pride. Just try and blacken it with your blazing batons, shotguns, and tear gas canisters. I'm ready.

A police officer in a feverish tone told me to move. I said, "*Chale*, this is my park." Before I knew it my face was being smeared into the dirt, a throbbing in my head. Officers pulled my arms back, handcuffing me. On the ground, drops of red slid over blades of green. By then the battle of Laguna Park had burst open. Bodies scurried in all directions. Through the tear gas mist could be seen shadows of children crying, women yelling, and people on the grass, kicking and gouging as officers thrust black jacks into ribs and spines. Several people tried to run into the yards and living rooms of nearby homes. Deputies followed in a murderous frenzy, pulling people out of back yards and porches.

A deputy pushed me into the back of a squad car. Somebody lay next to me, his hair oiled with blood. I didn't want to look for fear his brains were coming out. I managed to give him a piece of my shirt, my favorite, soon to be soaked. From the

East LA jail, where we were crowded into a holding tank for hours, we went on long rides to the Los Angeles County Jail, to juvenile hall, and county jail again. At one point, while we sat chained to one another in a county jail bus, officers sprayed mace into the windows; it burned our skin, eyes.

There were three other young dudes with me: Another 16-year-old, a 15-year-old, and his 13-year-old brother. They put us in with the adults—with murder, drug, and rape suspects. But nobody bothered us. There was an uprising outside and we were part of it. One guy recalled the Watts uprising and shook our hands. At one point, deputies took the four of us to the Hall of Justice, known as the Glasshouse. They threw us into "murderers row," where hardcore youth offenders and murder suspects were awaiting trial or serving time. I had a cell next to Charles Manson.

I was placed with a dude who had killed a teacher and another who had shot somebody in the Aliso Village housing projects. At first the dudes threatened me, pressing a stashed blade to my neck. But I knew, no matter what, never show fear. Soon we played cards, told jokes and stories. That night we heard that the "East LA riot" (this is what the media was calling it!) had escalated through much of Whittier Boulevard. Stores were being burned, looted. Police had killed people. Fires flared in other communities like Wilmington and Venice.

Then a radio reporter announced that Chicano journalist Ruben Salazar had been killed in a bar by sheriff's deputies. Salazar had been a lone voice in the existing media (he was a former Los Angeles Times reporter and KMEX-TV news director) for the Mexican people's struggle in the United States. Now silenced. At word of his death, the tier exploded into an uproar of outrage. Inmates gave out yells and rattled the cell bars.

47

For five days, I disappeared. My parents searched for me throughout the criminal justice system. They checked for my name in court records and arrest sheets. Nothing. Finally, in the middle of night, a guard awakened me, pulled me out of the cell and led me down brightly-lit corridors. Through a small thick-glassed window I saw my mother's weary face. When they finally brought me out, with dirt and caked blood on my clothes, she smiled—a lovely smile. I remember telling her, "I ain't no criminal, ma." She looked at me and replied, "I know, *mijo*, I know."

THE ROOSTER WHO THOUGHT
IT WAS A DOG

Echo Park mornings came on the wings
of a rooster's gnawing squawk.
This noise, unfortunately, also brought in
the afternoon, evenings, and most
hours of the day.
The rooster had no sense of time
nor any desire to commit to one.
He cock-a-doodled whenever he had the notion.
For late sleepers, day sleepers,
or your plain, ordinary,
run-of-the-mill night sleepers,
annoyance had this rooster's beak.
It was enough to drive one crazy.
Often I opened my back window
that faced the alley just across
from the backyard where the rooster
made his home.
"Shut up, or I'll blow your stinkin'
brains out," I'd yell.
Great communication technique.
It worked on the brats next door.
But the rooster never flinched.
With calm aplomb it continued to squawk.
For one thing, the rooster never gave out
a bonafide cock-a-doodle.
It sort of shouted it out.
It happened that the rooster lived
with three dogs: a German Shepherd and two mutts.
The dogs barked through their existence.
They barked at everything in sight.
I finally concluded the rooster

thought it was a dog.
Somehow, I didn't mind the dogs barking,
but when a rooster barks...that's murder.
In fact, I often saw it running alongside
the dogs as they raced across the dirt yard
barking at passing cars and people.
If the dogs went left, the rooster went left.
They'd go right, and dang if the rooster
didn't go right as well.
Now I don't know if this is a regular condition
for roosters. I thought I had a story for
the "Weekly World News." I could see it now:
The Rooster Who Thinks It's a Dog.
Who knows what rooster dementia we had here?
And whether the rooster chased cats up trees
or pissed on fire hydrants was not clear.
Once I grasped the heart of the matter,
I began to see the rooster in another light.
I almost felt sorry for this fowl
with an identity problem.
I wondered how it must react when its
owners threw chicken bones to the dogs.
Would it nibble on the remains
of its favorite hen?
I shuddered at the thought.
Yet despite the revelation of the rooster's bark,
the problem of sleep didn't end.
Then one day a new neighbor, a young lady,
who often drank herself to bliss,
got a gun and blew the rooster away.
She became somewhat of a local hero.
I must say, though, it was an unfitting end
for the bird.
But I suppose, one can tolerate barking dogs.
But barking roosters?
...that's another matter altogether.

ALWAYS RUNNING

ALWAYS RUNNING

All night vigil.
My two-and-a-half-year-old boy
and his 10-month-old sister
lay on the same bed,
facing opposite ends;
their feet touching.
They looked soft, peaceful,
bundled there in strands of blankets.
I brushed away roaches that meandered
across their faces,
but not even that could wake them.
Outside, the dark cover of night tore
as daybreak bloomed like a rose
on a stem of thorns.
I sat down on the backsteps,
gazing across the yellowed yard.
A 1954 Chevy Bel-Air stared back.
It was my favorite possession.
I hated it just then.
It didn't start when I tried to get it going
earlier that night. It had a bad solenoid.
I held a 12-gauge shotgun across my lap.
I expected trouble from the Paragons gang
of the west Lynwood *barrio.*
Somebody said I drove the car
that dudes from *Colonia Watts* used
to shoot up the Paragons' neighborhood.
But I got more than trouble that night.
My wife had left around 10 p.m.
to take a friend of mine home.
She didn't come back.
I wanted to kill somebody.
At moments, it had nothing to do

with the Paragons.
It had to do with a woman I loved.
But who to kill? Not her—
sweet allure wrapped in a black skirt.
I'd kill myself first.
Kill me first?
But she was the one who quit!
Kill her? No, think man! I was hurt, angry...
but to kill her? To kill a Paragon?
To kill anybody?
I went into the house
and put the gun away.

Later that morning, my wife came for her things:
some clothes, the babies...their toys.
A radio, broken TV, and some dishes remained.
I didn't stop her.
There was nothing to say that my face
didn't explain already.
Nothing to do...but run.

So I drove the long haul to Downey
and parked near an enclosed area
alongside the Los Angeles River.
I got out of the car,
climbed over the fence
and stumbled down the slopes.
A small line of water rippled in the middle.
On rainy days this place flooded and flowed,
but most of the time it was dry
with dumped garbage and dismembered furniture.
Since a child, the river and its veins of canals
were places for me to think. Places to heal.
Once on the river's bed, I began to cleanse.
I ran.

I ran into the mist of morning,
carrying the heat of emotion
through sun's rays;
I ran past the factories
that lay smack in the middle
of somebody's backyard.
I ran past alleys with overturned trashcans
and mounds of tires.
Debris lay underfoot. Overgrown weeds
scraped my leg as I streamed past;
recalling the song of bullets
that whirred in the wind.

I ran across bridges, beneath overhead passes,
and then back alongside the infested walls
of the concrete river;
splashing rainwater as I threaded,
my heels colliding against the pavement.
So much energy propelled my legs
and, just like the river,
it went on for miles.

When all was gone,
the concrete river
was always there
and me, always running.

COLOMBIAN STAR

Oh, Colombian star,
I reach out to you
From between bedsheets,
Through dark corridors—
From outside of frosty windows.

You are the luminance of Latin woman,
Yet your silence repels embraces;
A barricade against intrusions.

You provoke sleepless nights,
Drenching me in a downpour
Of indecisions.

Come, talk to me.

Talk to me of your terrors—
Of a seclusion with child and hunger,
Of a trusting shattered by the one
You most desired.

Talk to me of love,
Which you had so much to give.
Of your "sacred" emotions;
How immutable time and clenched fists
Battered them.

Let me help carry
The weight of your escapes.

Let them go!
Let the memories come hurtling,
        of an alcoholic, enraged lover

with a shotgun to your neck
who forced you into humiliations
I can't even imagine.

Speak, so we can wade
In languid conversation,
Share soft touches,
Seek careless joys.

Oh, Colombian star,
Burning from a distance,
Remember, yes,
But everything.

WAITING

What made the waiting so painful?
The woman had called; she was
on her way.
Tense, I waited, sitting at the kitchen table.

There had been too many nights
        waking up to bottles
        and books on the floor;
        two small children parked on
        blankets in a corner.

Alone ain't so bad.

Dreams of women yet to be touched,
        to be smelled. It ain't bad.

Up on a hill, hidden by wood-and-shingle
shacks alongside curbless roads, visited by nobody
        unless they had to be here.

Alone ain't so bad.

Hammering holes into walls with fists.
Tears streaming down my face at saxophone riffs.
Looking at old photos, feeding babies,
taking out trash and thinking of her.

It ain't so bad. I couldn't stand it.

Looked through personal ads in the weeklies.
Made phone calls. Wrote letters. Came across
Video-Date; "The Godsend for Lonely People."
I called after three false starts. Lady said

she would be here Saturday.
It's Saturday and I'm going nuts.

An hour finding the place (an old stucco-white
basement room. You can't miss it. *Cholo* graffiti
on the front door).

She came, made her pitch, saw the hurt in my eyes
(I always spoke with my eyes, damn it), a longing
for sweet companionship—not of drunken homeboys
or angel-dusted street women. For the mother
of my kids;
>   out at Sonny's Lounge, sucking Kahluas and
>   highballs, and shooting out wicked smiles
>   at discoed-out dudes.

The lady looked at my eyes, and then stopped.

Refused to sell me the Video-Date.
Refused to take the check.

"This can't help you," she said—and walked out.

BLACK MEXICAN

"The worst thing you can do is fall in love with a whore."
                                                    —a homeboy
"...but she's a woman."
                        —me

The girl appeared through the red haze
of stage lights, a black Mexican
who told her family in Acapulco she was working
in Tijuana cleaning homes when in fact
she sold herself to sailors and tourists
reconquering the people on weekends.

She came to me, her small frame leaning
against a table, all of 15 years,
dark eyes shining through smoke.
Or I came to her, a teenaged runaway from *Lomas*,
hitchhiking into the void of antiquity,
needing more than the empty stares
of sunlight in the mirror.
Or she came to me, yearning for this dance
and the wraith of real love.

She walked up
with dreams of America
and yellowed teeth.
She came in the caricature of a voice,
with motherhood
sliced across her belly
and eyes of hiding in mud fields
as family sounds
closed in on her, carnivorous like dogs,
murmuring about how pretty she is,
how it doesn't hurt,
and the fathers,

the uncles
the brothers,
all slamming into her
until she could squeeze into herself
and die.

Across the way was a hotel of cracked plaster.
Its hallways echoed with the shouts of drunken boys,
blond like Ohio,
who scraped off the Tijuana women
from the soles of their feet.

We crossed the street
with the asphalt erupting beneath us
and folded into a hotel room.
She undressed,
revealing the skin of ancient tribes;
still fighting, still bleeding.
I lay on the bed.
Told her no.
Told her yes.
Told her I had no money.
She looked at me as if sorry.
We exchanged fingers
then kissed, and I cried,
kissed and cried into the moments
of my first suckling.

THE BULL'S EYE INN

(Apologies to T.S. Eliot for the first two lines)

Let us go then,
you and I,
to the Bull's Eye Inn,
through the rusted iron gates
into the dark and damp, stepping on saw-dusted
floors gushing with ether, where my ex-wife
once waited tables on weekends grinning with death.
Come to where the blood, beer, and barf
flowed with the bourbon washes.

My ex-wife often invited me to watch over her.
My job on those weekends, she explained,
was to sit in a dark corner, by myself,
and keep the out-of-work mechanics,
the foundrymen
and slow-talking *cholos*
from going too far—
which was like blowing a balloon
and trying to stop just before it burst!

Dudes would buy her drinks
and she brought the drinks over to me.
Laid back against a plush seat,
I silently toasted
their generosity.

I did a toast to her too, to our babies,
to the blood-shot eyes of East LA nights
and the midnight romps we once had,
near naked, in the park.

Many times in the candle-lit haze,
as a disc jockey played tunes
behind a chain-link barrier,
the bullets came flying and the beer bottles
crashed on the wall behind my head.

Once on the dance floor some dude
smacked his old lady to the ground.
Later that night she returned,
firing a .22 handgun into the bar
—and missing everybody—
as Little Willie G. crooned "Sad Girl"
from a turntable.

Con artists congregated here,
including the Earl of Lincoln Heights
who once sold a house he didn't own.

And boys with tattoos and scars crisscrossing skin,
prowled the pool tables, passing bills,
while trying to out-hustle each other
as disco beats and *cumbias* pulled people
onto the lopsided dance floor.

My ex-wife danced too.
I watched dudes hold her, kiss her neck,
eye her behind
and look down
her sweaty breasts.

But I also knew this was the closest
I would ever get to her anymore,
in that dark corner,
with beer bottles rising from a table—
when she needed me.

Outside the Bull's Eye Inn
the hurting never stopped.

Outside the Bull's Eye Inn
we locked into hate
shrouded in the lips of love.

Outside the Bull's Eye Inn
we had two children
who witnessed our drunken brawls—
my boy once entered our room,
and danced and laughed with tears in his eyes
to get us to stop.

But inside, beside the blaze of bar lights,
she was the one who stole into my sleep,
the one who fondled my fears,
the one who inspired
the lust of honeyed remembrance.

She was the song of regret behind a sudden smile.

DON'T READ THAT POEM!

(For Patricia Smith)

She rises from a chair
and slides toward the stage
with satin feet over a worn-wood floor.
She bears down on the microphone
like a blues singer about to reveal
some secrets.
A fever of poems in her hand.
She seizes the mike
and begins her seduction.

I'm in the back of the bar,
my head down.
The things she does to me
with words.
I want to leave. I want her
never to begin.
She starts with a poem
about Daddy-love, and I feel
like getting up right there
and yelling: Don't read that poem!
That one that causes little bursts
of screams inside my head,
that makes tears come to my eyes,
that I refuse to let fall.

Don't read that poem!
the one about a daughter raped and killed
in the shadow of a second's dark fury.
I want to hide in the neon glare above me;
to swim away in the glass of beer
I hold close to me.
She does another poem

about her many mouths
and I want to howl:
Don't read that poem!
that one that entices me
to crawl under her skin,
to be her heartbeat.

Oh, how she plunks the right notes,
rendering me as clay in bruised hands.
No, don't do the one about
what it is to be
a nine-year-old black girl,
the truth of it trembling at my feet.
Somebody should make her stop!

I should be home, watching TV,
blank-eyed behind stale headlines,
cold popcorn on the couch,
a dusty turntable
going round and round and round.
I should be fixing a car.
Or shooting eight-ball.
But I can't leave.
I need to taste the salt of her soliloquy,
to be drunk with the sobriety
of her verse
quaking beneath my eyelids.

JAROCHO BLUES

You came with long, luxurious hair,
black as the deep tint of heart-blood,
      almost blue.

You came with a smile and a guitar,
groping for a song:
      Una nueva cancion.
      Exitos de Augustín Lara.
      A *Jarocho* blues.

You came with a tequila bottle
and sat cross-legged on a rug of colors.
I watched and you sang,
the lit air carrying a litany
      of women's stories.
Your voice like a silk veil
      over dripping candles,
bringing back family songs
      over *copas de vino.*
Your voice and the night of day.

A mahogany wood table held an overturned glass.
You sat next to it stretching the chords
over my eyes, strumming the strings
      into infinity.

You sang, and I fell into a notated dream
with a chorus of psalms drenching in sorrows.
You sang, and the bougainvilleas of youth
      came to me in torrents.
You sang, and tears cut paths down the wall,
blanketing me in a spell of ointments.
You sang, and the tequila burned

the edges of my mouth.
I never wanted it to end,
        your singing.
A guitar across your lap.
Your eyes closed.
Waves of hair over your shoulders
        with strands like spider webs
        across your face.

You sang, and I died.
Dead for all the broken men.
Dead for all who ever stopped believing.
Dead for all who ever thought women

Dead for all who ever hungered
to be touched
by the flesh
of such a voice.

LIPS

I sat in Chicago traffic
waiting for a light to change.
My fingers scored a rhythm
on top of the metal door
while faces stared down
from third-floor bay windows.
Not to intrude, but from behind a blue Toyota,
I spotted them. Lips.
Perfect, red, with thin creases
and slightly opened.
Lips like candy
encased in a rectangular side-view mirror.
My car was just behind the Toyota.
The back of a woman's head in front of me.
But in the mirror just lips, enormous
as they rubbed the sides of the plastic rim.
The lips took off after the next green.
I pressed the accelerator,
unmindful of the old lady trying
to cross the street
with bags on both arms.
I was compelled to look at those lips
even as they rushed through a yellow light
forcing me to risk the red.
The lips carried with them
the soul of skin,
the summer of a smile...taking me home.
Lips like being cradled in a soft rain,
making me do a perfect backflip
into wet memory.
Lips whispering into my ear,
licking the side of my mouth—
hiding secrets behind honeyed faces.

It didn't matter what the woman looked like.
She had lips.
Then the turn signals flashed
and lips made a left-hand turn.
I continued on over the ruptured streets,
thinking of lips
through the flames of afternoon traffic.

MUSIC OF THE MILL

MUSIC OF THE MILL

On Slauson Avenue, the red-orange ingots of molten steel sat in rows on gondola cars near the soaking pits. An overhead crane with huge iron jaws lifted each ingot and maneuvered it into a conveyor system leading into the 32-inch forge. Standing across the street, one could feel the heat.

Inside the mill, men in various colored hard hats moved around like so many ants. Each one was part of another; each with his own task. Mechanics and electricians strolled on catwalks repairing machinery and power lines. Another building down, the electric furnaces rumbled without end. At certain intervals, a furnace would be tipped over by huge hydraulic legs to pour out a ladle of molten slag onto a gray transport car to be railed away.

Friday was pay day and the Slauson Avenue hotels, bars, and stores recovered from a week-long hangover. A small stucco shed on the parking lot of a liquor store cashed the men's checks, but not before taking from one to ten percent of the net, depending on the overtime. Racing forms were scattered around the line of men. Painted women from the hotels took positions nearby to offer what they could do for the night. The neon on the bars proclaimed the latest "mill-special" price for drinks. By the time many of the men got home, they didn't have much left to show for the double shifts and rotating turns. Many of them failed to find a wife or the kids when they finally entered their house.

Blacks and Latinos filled the lower-paid labor crews. And they often made up the mill hands on the forge. The better paying jobs, especially the skilled crafts, belonged to mostly whites. One of these guys was a man named Denton. He was a red-faced, Southern-bred millwright with about thirty years' time in the mill. Denton headed a group of local Ku Klux Klanners. The ones in the plant would go to union meetings to disrupt any effort by other workers to better their conditions. Denton was responsible for having a number of dudes fired. He was close to the company bosses. He was a hero to the older white mechanics.

I recall the time I had just been hired as an oiler-greaser. It was such a feat that I walked around the house for days in an unscuffed hard hat and greaseless tool belt. There were only a handful of minorities in the oil gang then: a black, two Mexicans, an Indian, a Puerto Rican, and a Colombian. White oiler-greasers usually required from two weeks to a couple of months to move up into the repair crews; it took me three years.

Not that I wasn't capable of the work. I even taught many of the dudes who moved up before I did. And the other minorities were great mechanics, especially Izzie, the Puerto Rican, who never moved up. He eventually quit after years of "good service." The Colombian went back to the old country. The black dude had to join an alcoholics group after he almost killed himself on the furnace floor following a two-week binge. And the Indian just vanished one day.

I finally made millwright's helper on the electric furnaces. One day I saw Denton look down from a railing on top of an overhead crane he was working on. He was some forty feet above the 10-inch mill. Denton's hard hat was long without sheen, all scratched and dusty. His blue eyes glazed like the electric spark of an arc weld. He said little, but he watched everything. Denton spotted me as I worked replacing a brass bearing. I knew why. Denton served as the company's eyes. He had one guy thrown out of the plant because Denton said he was sleeping beneath the shears. He particularly fingered those men who spoke out, who refused to succumb to the mill bosses.

Denton made obvious his hatred of blacks. He talked about their easy manner, how their skin glistened in the heat of battle with steel. Denton also hated the dusk-faced Latins, their steady demeanor, and the strange language that grated against his Southern-bred sensibilities. The minorities sang too much, laughed too much; always too quick with a word. Denton saw himself as the guardian of American right. He protected the confederate ideals, the white way of life. Yet to most of us, his family was no different than those foreign-tongued immigrants, Cherokees, and Mississippi men he scorned. But he was a millwright. He knew his craft. He used his brains. He was no lowly laborer. He was a knight of the forge. He was above them all, always from a view on a crane. He slung his tools over his shoulders and walked the mill like he owned it, as if it didn't own him. The mill was his goddess. The furnaces' spew, his children. He was protector, brother...lover. For thirty years he mended its machinery. What would it be without him? And then these blacks, Mexicans, and Indians come along who don't know the meaning of work. They're all leeches. They only take, but won't give any more than they have to. From his metal perch, he saw that they paid for their "crimes."

The company loved Denton. The union would never be a challenge as long as men like Denton dominated it. There was a link between the steel mill owners and Denton. The same blood seemed to flow between them. Only one owned the mill, and the other acted as its prison guard.

But the mill knew no chivalry. It was a cold lover who fails to recognize you the next day after a sweat-and-blood night. It was a mother who denies her babes suckling. It turned to dust everything it encountered, spitting it back as steel bars, plates, and beams.

One day, Denton was working beneath the skids of the 32-inch mill when all of a sudden he climbed out, gasping and giving out guttural moans through a bluish mouth. He grabbed at air, fell on his knees, and clutched at his chest. He tried to hold onto a shaft and coupling in front of him, but his fingers, stubby from years of being banged on, only smeared the grease.

One of the new laborers saw Denton's collapse. The dude dropped a shovel of oil and metal flakes and ran to assist Denton, who squirmed on the ground, an incoherent sound rising from his throat. Just then a handful of workers stepped in front of the new dude. They looked at him and shook their heads. The dude knew what this meant: Leave the KKK man alone, let his death rattle be the music the mill gives back for treachery. As Denton gasped a last time, the mill he lived for, that carried his dreams along with the pipes and shafts, the mill that destroyed lives so he could keep his privilege, began to belch back his stench. It began to throw up the years of lies and fingering and turning his back to hands that reached out to him.

The new guy looked as if he had to do something. "He's dying," he screamed. "We got to help him!" But all he got were icy gazes from beneath stained hard hats, the muscles of brown and black skin rippling below drenched shirts. The look of no. "It ends here," a mill hand said.

Flames thrust out of opened tuyeres. Gears ripped and rattled as red, malleable steel bars thundered down rolls of conveyors through dies of several sizes. Slag flew everywhere. Denton was laid out, stretched and spread-eagled on his back. It was how he saw his last light. The row of men in front of the new dude slowly dispersed. Tears streamed down the dude's face.

Elsewhere there was no sorrow. The years of midnight abductions by hooded men, a hemp rope squeezed around a daddy's neck, losing work with the eyes of a hungry child tearing into skin—that pain died on the floor of the 32-inch mill. This was the mill's payback, steel's vendetta, the justice that churned when all else failed.

JESUS SAVES

This dude *Jesús Saves*
must be popular or something:
You see his name everywhere.
I first saw it when I woke up
from a Bunker Hill cardboard box
to a huge sign near the top
of the LA library.
It read: "*Jesús Saves*."

I wish I were that guy...
then I wouldn't be
this chocked-faced pirate on city
seas, this starved acrobat of the alcoves
loitering against splintered doors.
Then I wouldn't be this aberration
who once had a home, made of stone even,
and a woman to call wife.
In the old country,
I worked since I was seven!
I knew the meaning
of the sun's behest
for pores to weep.
But now such toil is allowed
to rot like too many berries on a bush.

In the old country, I laughed the loudest,
made the most incisive remarks
and held at bay even the most
limpid of gatherings.

But here I am a grieving poet,
a scavenger of useless literature;
they mean nothing in this place...

my metaphoric manner,
the spectacle of my viscous verse
—nothing!
I am but a shadow on the sidewalk,
a spot of soot on a block wall;
a roll of dice tossed across
a collapsing hallway in a downtown
SRO hotel.

Ok, *Señor Saves*, right now this is your time.
But someday a billboard
will proclaim my existence.
Someday people will sigh my name
as if it were confection on the lips.
As long as I have a rhythm in my breast,
there will come this fine day
when this orphan, pregnant with genius,
is discovered sprouting epiphanies like wings
on the doorstep of
mother civilization.

THE BLAST FURNACE

A foundry's stench, the rolling mill's clamor,
the jackhammer's concerto leaving traces
between worn ears. Oh sing me a bucket shop blues
under an accordion's spell
with blood notes cutting through the black air
for the working life, for the rotating shifts,
for the day's diminishment and rebirth.
The lead seeps into your skin like rainwater
along stucco walls; it blends into the fabric of cells,
the chemistry of bone, like a poisoned paintbrush
coloring skies of smoke, devouring like a worm
that never dies, a fire that's never quenched.
The blast furnace bellows out a merciless melody
as molten metal runs red down your back,
as assembly lines continue rumbling
into your brain, into forever,
while rolls of pipes crash onto brick floors.
The blast furnace spews a lava of insipid dreams,
a deathly swirl of screams; of late night wars
with a woman, a child's book of fear,
a hunger of touch, a hunger of poetry,
a daughter's hunger for laughter.
It is the sweat of running, of making love,
a penitence pouring into ladles of slag.
It is falling through the eyes of a whore,
a red-core bowel of rot,
a red-eyed train of refugees,
a red-scarred hand of unforgiveness,
a red-smeared face of spit.
It is blasting a bullet through your brain,
the last dying echo of one who enters
the volcano's mouth to melt.

CARRYING MY TOOLS

Any good craftsman carries his tools.
Years ago, they were always at the ready.
In the car. In a knapsack.
Claw hammers, crisscrossed heads,
32 ouncers. Wrenches in all sizes,
sometimes with oil caked on the teeth.
Screwdrivers, with multicolored
plastic handles
(what needed screwing got screwed).
I had specialty types: Allen wrenches,
torpedo levels, taps and dies.
A trusty tape measure.
Maybe a chalk line.
Millwrights also carried dial indicators,
micrometers—the precision kind.
They were cherished like a fine car,
a bottle of rare wine,
or a moment of truth.
I believed that anyone could survive
without friends, without the comfort of blankets
or even a main squeeze
(for a short while anyway).
But without tools...now there was hard times.
Without tools, what kind of person could I be?
The tools were my ticket to new places.
I often met other travelers, their tools in tow,
and I'd say: "Go ahead, take my stereo and TV.
Take my car. Take my toys of leisure.
Just leave the tools."
Nowadays, I don't haul these mechanical implements.
But I still make sure to carry the tools
of my trade: Words and ideas,

the kind no one can take away.
So there may not be any work today,
but when there is, I'll be ready.
I got my tools.

HEAVY TELLS A STORY

When Heavy tells a story
the millwright shanty under the electric furnaces
chokes with quiet, amid the roar,
as Heavy pauses, adjusts his mountainous weight
over a creaky grease-stained metal chair
and looks up at the whirling ceiling fan
next to fluorescent lights hanging by wires.
His fingers lace like so many sausages
across the canvas of blue workshirt
on his chest.

Heavy tells his story
and the voice of reason quickens the demise
of foulness from red-faced millwrights
just back from a repair job
and sitting around for the five air whistles
that again call them to combat on the furnace floor.

All laughter stops, all nonsense sayings
and cuts of wisdom cease their echo
when Heavy tells a story.

Heavy talks about the Mexican melter
who once had an affair with the Pit Boss's wife.
The heart of the problem—and the fact
from which the story's plot revolves—
was that the melter lived across the street
from the Pit Boss.
One night just before the graveyard shift,
the melter left his home, kissed his wife's
round face and proceeded to walk to the bus stop.

But a bullet pierced through his hardhat
and he fell, like an overturned stack of fire bricks,
onto the pavement.

The moral of this story:
Never have an affair with someone
whose old man lives
within shooting distance.

Heavy tells a story
about a furnace foreman who always yelled
at the laborers for failing to clean
the bag house of the built-up filth
from hours of cooking scrap iron and ore.
The men told him it was too dangerous
to walk on the tin-roofed panels;
their weight could cause
them to fall some 30 feet
into the gaping mouth of a flaming furnace below.
"Nonsense," the foreman yelled,
"you're all just lazy Polacks."
(he called everyone Polacks).
The foreman then proceeded to walk
across the roof as the men stood nearby,
with mouths open, near the safety of side beams.
"You see," he said standing in the middle
as hydraulics moved shutters
up and down to capture the sulphur dust.

Then the foreman moved forward
and before anyone could shout,
he crashed through the roof,
screaming into a reddened pot of molten metal;
the oxygen in his body making popping sounds
as it entered. The furnace operators continued
to pour ladles of scrap iron and to melt the steel.

They skimmed the slag off the top
and when it was ready, they poured
the molten mass into ingot molds.

There was nothing they could do for the foreman,
they said. Production had to keep going.

Heavy looks into the eyes of his listeners and says:
Somewhere there's a skyscraper in downtown LA
with steel beams made from the ingot
with the foreman's body in it.
Somewhere there's a bridge or underground pipe
with the man's remains chemically bound
within the molecular structure.

Heavy tells a story...

and the men lay down their tools,
the coffee is poured into heavy ceramic cups,
the shanty stills beneath the rumbling,
and even foremen stop by
to pay a listen
when Heavy tells a story.

FIRST DAY OF WORK

My dark-eyed wife
saw me off in the new
green work clothes.
Me—proud in shiny hard hat
and steel-tipped shoes.

First day of work.
What a day! What a dream.
Our *barrio Florencia* flat
never ached so good.

Days before this place stunk
of newlywed poor.
I couldn't find work.
Oh, I had tried:
Trouncing the rows
of factories,
warehouses,
and construction sites.

Come back next month,
          they'd say.
You ain't got experience,
          they'd say.
How the hell was I
supposed to get some,
          I'd say.

She was tired. I was tired.
We were tired of each other.
Then a friend of a friend,
who I met standing in line
for an application one morning,

told me to check out
the construction site
on Alameda Street near Wilmington.

I went. I was tired.

Then they called back. Great day!
They needed helpers. They needed
young backs like mine
to haul and pull and drag.
I'm your man. For sure!

I got the shoes: the Sears workingman's special.
I borrowed the money...but hey,
I was working again.

So off I went. Kinda nervous.
My wife almost looked happy.

I worked with a journeyman
millwright; putting together
a conveyor system—a whirl
of gears, electric motors,
rubber belts, and hoses
full of oil.

At one point he had to arc-weld
two pieces of metal.
Hold this for me while I weld,
        he said.

Okay. Anything. I can do it.
It was great, watching that
little sun glow on the steel,
fusing it with another rod
held in an electric claw.

It looked sharp, bright
—powerful.

Lunch came. Jokes about new dudes,
Mexicans, blacks—
I didn't know what to say, but hey,
it was work.

Most of the day went fine.
But then came a burning in my eyes.
I tried to ignore it.
But something tore at them
from the inside.

I didn't know what to do.
I told the journeyman, finally,
when I couldn't see
the end of the crescent wrench
I was pulling on.

Did you look at the spark
when I was welding?
          he asked.
Well, yeah...

Damn it, man!
          he shouted.
Don't you know not to look
at an arc-weld!

Great. My first day at work
and I could go blind.

The pain became unbearable.
Every time I exposed the eyes,
the sting, like fire,

cut through them.
That afternoon
my dark-eyed wife
came for me.

At the industrial clinic,
I got the official word:
I had seared the lubrication
off the eyes—
that precious oil that protected
the sensitive cornea and iris
from dirt and debris.

Without this, I felt
every hint of dust, lint, smog
slicing into me.

First day of work!

That evening, I lay cradled
in my wife's arms;
my eyes in bandages.

THEY COME TO DANCE

An aged, bondo-scarred Buick
pushes dust around its wheels
as it slithers up Brooklyn Avenue
toward La Tormenta, bar and dance club.

The Buick pulls up to clutter
along a cracked sidewalk
beneath a street lamp's yellow luminance.
A man and a woman, in their late 30s,
pour out of a crushed side door.

They come to dance.

The man wears an unpressed suit and baggy pants:
K-Mart specials.
She is overweight
in a tight blue dress.
The slits up the side
reveal lace and panty hose.

They come with passion-filled bodies,
factory-torn like *ropa vieja*.
They come to dance the workweek away
as a soft rain begins to buffet
the club's steamed windows.

Women in sharp silk dresses and harsh,
painted-on makeup crowd the entrance.
Winos stare at the women's flight across
upturned streets
and up wooden stairs.

Men in slacks and cowboy shirts
or cheap polyester threads
walk alone or in pairs.

¿Oye compa, que pues?
Aquí no más, de oquis..."

Outside La Tormenta's doors
patrons line up to a van dispensing tacos
while a slightly-opened curtain
reveals figures gyrating
to a beat bouncing off strobe-lit walls.

They come to dance
and remember
the way flesh feels flush
against a cheek
and how a hand opens slightly,
shaped like a seashell,
in the small
of a back.

They come to dance
and forget
the pounding hum
of an assembly line,
while the boss' grating throat
tells everyone to go back to work
over the moans of a woman
whose finger dangles
in a glove.

They come to dance:
Former peasants. Village kings.
City squatters. High-heeled princesses.

The man and woman lock the car doors
and go through La Tormenta's weather-stained
curtain leading into
curling smoke.

Inside the Buick are four children.
They press their faces
against the water-streaked glass
and cry through large eyes;
mirrors of a distant ocean.

BETHLEHEM NO MORE

(For Bruce S.)

Bethlehem Steel's
shift-turn whistles
do not blast out
in Maywood anymore.

Mill workers no longer congregate
at Slauson Avenue bars
on pay day.

Bethlehem's soaking pits
are frigid now.

Mill families,
once proud and comfortable,
now gather for unemployment checks
or food.

Bethlehem,
I never thought you would be missed.
When we toiled under the girders,
we cursed your name.

But you were bread on the table;
another tomorrow.

My babies were born
under the Bethlehem health plan.
My rent was paid
because of those long and humid
days and nights.

I recall being lowered
into oily and greasy pits
or standing unsteady
on two-inch beams
thirty feet in the air
and wondering if I would survive
to savor another weekend.

I recall my fellow workers
who did not survive—
burned alive from caved-in furnace roofs
or severed in two by burning red steel rods—
while making your production quotas.

But Bethlehem you are no more.
We have made you rich;
rich enough to take our toil
and invest it elsewhere.

Rich enough
to make us poor again.

A HARVEST OF EYES

A HARVEST OF EYES

A street finds its song in the murmur
of a woman's heart as she lies on the sidewalk.
Conversations in concrete promise nothing.
The rustling of vines along an unkept lawn
is a man finding a place to sleep.
The ruin of hype is in the lined face of a former carpenter,
here among a harvest of eyes
uttering truth in liquid voices,
eyes like multicolored pearls submerged beneath
tears frozen by wind. They are wondrous spheres
shimmering with a faint sparkle, smoldering
with pain...yet distant. The distance between cracks
on cement, the distance of a layoff slip,
the distance of the hungry next to the fed.
You hate them, you pity them, but don't get near them.
The geography of politics. Here is a war vet,
a father of wiry boys, whose auto plant job
crumbled after 18 years of service. Look deeply,
see yourself in the jagged lines
of a severed America, where once the tilled
stalks of wheat watercolored the horizons,
where once steel reigned amid the toppled timbers,
where a homecoming queen could stand tall
on a platform, a proud papa at her side,
and have it mean something—not this occupied
corner in a carnival of neon shadows
on fractured walls, not this bristling yield of eyes,
like ripened fruit, ready to be plucked.

THE QUEST FOR FLIGHT

A *boricua* brother once took his wife and me
to visit her parents at an East Harlem
housing project. After we parked, we entered
the chatter of lives in granite, of old
men playing dominos, of children and
children and children, crossing the littered street
into their world of unlikely,
super-powered heroes in a quest for flight.

We stood in front of a 13-story building,
a monument of decayed schemes, of failed
charity; a tall chipped structure that is
supposed to be home. But jail bars greeted us.
Hypodermic needles got kicked out of the way.
And mustached boys leaned against tussled-
haired girls as a little Willie Colon blared
a trombone that bounced fragments of notes
off the cracked wallboard in the corridor.

We took a mean-spirited elevator
to the 10th floor. All the doors looked alike;
the stained walls could have been
the housing projects of Ramona Gardens
or Aliso Village in East L.A.
I noticed this about the federally-
subsidized homes I'd been to—whether
in LA, Denver, Chicago, or East Harlem:
they may look different from the outside,
but inside most of them looked the same.

A middle-aged man greeted us, smiling large
and waving us in as if we were a kind wind
on a scorched day. A gray-haired woman shuffled

in the kitchen. As we entered, she began
to relate the latest *chisme* to her daughter.
The man took my arm to a table where he
displayed a bottle of Mescal. He explained
how he learned to drink Mescal after having
gone to Korea and fought with Mexicans in the war.
Personally, I said, give me dark rum.

Dinner came and, again, as if in my honor,
enchiladas were served. I liked Mexican food,
but I suggested that their culture didn't have
to be displaced for my sake. "Please,
I get this every day," I said. "Let's enjoy
what you enjoy. Let me have some black beans
and rice with *pice*. How about *lenchón y salsa*
de bacalao?

As we ate, I looked out at the Central Park
jungle that sat lush in the middle of countless
leaning, window-scarred buildings. Then in
the midst of cuisine and conversation, something,
a body, streaked down outside the window.
My *compañero's* wife yelled out.
"Somebody fell!" We pushed aside the chairs,
rushed to the window and looked below,
but couldn't see anything.

My partner and I raced down the 10 floors
to a crowd gathering on a grassy knoll.
The police were already there.
They held back people as I approached a cop
to ask questions. He told me to get lost.
But a sergeant nearby offered what he knew.

It was a suicide, he said,
a 27-year-old man
who had just been released from a mental institution.

His mother had called police
saying her son was threatening to jump.
But when they arrived, there was only
a broken body on a cement walkway
and a woman, some 13 floors up,
screaming.

THE NEWS
YOU DON'T GET AT HOME

The news you don't get at home
is in the dangling flesh of peasants and workers,
in the silenced tongues of poets and journalists,
in the machine-gunned remains of women and children.

The news you don't get at home
is molded, packaged, abbreviated,
synthesized, and castrated,
through the phone lines,
from the bleeding pens of eyeless stooges
who went to all the fine schools,
worked on all the fine newspapers,
who covered the great wars
("Hey, is this Lebanon or El Salvador?")
who wired in the fabrications to fit the ignorance,
who sat in small, dingy hotels with great scotch
and claimed to be truthsayers.

Somehow these "journalists" failed to see
the election fraud; the names of the dead
resurrected on election rosters
(and they say there are no miracles in this world!).
They failed to see the trucked-in thugs
from out of town
and the death threats carved on the inside
of a woman's thigh.

The news you don't get at home
is in the withered eye sockets
of emaciated faces, seeking food,
seeking redress, seeking emancipation—

oh, such a word!
It rarely makes the sweaty copy
of these "objective observers,"
these TV-bred, English 101-graduates
who know where the semicolons go
but who couldn't find the heart of humanity
in an outstretched hand.

CITY OF ANGELS

Somewhere out there, lies the city.
Bare-breasted. Awaiting my return.
The city of abandoned nights,
of six-year-olds falling through rusted fire escapes,
of welfare hotels in facades of diseased stone;
the city of grit, wood, and bone.

I step out of a foul-smelling Greyhound bus
into the mouth of a moistened dawn,
spraying its colors on cardboard "condos"
on the sidewalk.
Here I stroll, among the walking dead,
among the criminalized and displaced,
the sun of the desert our only roof,
the song of our wails,
the wails of our song,
thundering against the sides of this
city of angels
so far removed from heaven.

MEAN STREETS

(To Piri Thomas)

Your mean streets
visited my mean streets
one hollow summer day
in the 60s
and together we played ball,
cracking sounds on the asphalt
echoing from Los to Harlem.

And every time I shot dope into a vein,
you felt the euphoria in your prose
and I saw me in you
and I heard you yell
and it was my voice
tearing open the night sky.

Oh, so many times, I crumpled the pages
of your life to my face,
and cried:
Savior, Savior, hold my hand!

And your seven long times
was a long night for me,
but I knew you, *compadre*,
you, steady companion down the alleyways,
barrio brother,
father/partner...teacher.

I heard your screams
and entered through the gateway
of your nightmare
into the gateway of my dreams.

EVERY ROAD

Every road should come to this end:
A place called home.
When you don't have one
the expanse of sky is your roof,
the vast fields of green your living room.
Every city, your city.
When you speak, you speak for the country.
In the wrinkled faces and the sun-scarred eyes
mother earth calls us to fury.
Every child without a home
is everyone's child.
The daily murders go unanswered:
To die of cold in Southern California.
To starve in New York City,
the restaurant capital of the world.
To have no coat in the Broadway of coats.
The crimes pile up as high as the mountains
of grain that are warehoused and stored away
from those who need it.
A mother's child is taken away for neglect
because she can't pay rent
and eat at the same time.
Children born of a labor of love are condemned
for the lack of labor.
Mothers crawl through city veins
like blood on the grapevine.
Every road should come to this end.
A place called home.

CHAINED TIME

When history is stolen,
its heart wrenched from the meat of time,
it is like a missing orange-red mango
from a stained fruitbowl;
a still life of bruised apples, squashed grapes,
and brown bananas left behind.

History becomes that old DeSoto out in back
with peeling blue paint
and the parking-lot bondo job
coming apart in chucks;
weeds and foxtails hugging flattened tires.

It's a big brother who you admire
but who only comes around
to wrestle you to the ground.

History becomes a lost love in an old photograph;
still smiling, still with that look,
but fading like the colors,
the eyes—like the smile.

It is an old crescent wrench coming apart in sections:
A moss-covered anchor, a rusty machete
ready to slice into your head.
But when history is found—
because it may be stolen but nobody can destroy it—
it is a shiny new Excalibur
with a cloister of ivory horses on the handle,
beckoning like a gem in clear water,
to be held, to be swung, to render as it rises,
taking with it the fire, the purpose,

the dreams of humankind as a weapon
of chained time,
set free.

DON'T GO GENTLE
INTO THAT GOOD EXPRESSWAY

They say people in New York City are cold,
that they enter like the blackness of night
and rip into you when you shine with the
weakness of a smile. They say, you can't smile
in New York City because it could be
a death warrant. A kind word is a likely
ticket to a back-street mugging. Nobody
cares in New York City.

But I don't know...the city seemed refreshing
to me. People were upfront. They yelled,
they laughed, they had no qualms about your worth.
I could walk these streets and face anyone and be
crazier than the craziest dude
and ride the subways looking untouchable
and nobody knew whether to talk to me
or walk away. In most cities
madness seethes below the skin.
In New York City, it storms through the eyes.

And, at least once, New York City
showed me some heart.
I had entered a packed expressway when a bobtail
truck in front of me rammed into a stalled car.
Fire then flared out of the truck's hood.
The truck driver dove out the side window
onto the asphalt and struck his head.
As he lay unconscious, we all got out
of our cars; somebody ran to an emergency phone
to summon help.
The rest of us rushed over to the driver.
We looked at each other and figured if we

didn't move him, the truck could explode
and break up over his body. But to move him
meant the risk of getting sued,
a New Yorker reasoned next to me.

In the seconds that followed,
we decided that everyone there
would take a hold of the guy.
Somebody got an arm, another a leg...
one guy just placed a hand on the dude's chest.

We carried the truck driver to the side
of the road. An ambulance finally came.
We continued to stand by the dude
until they laid him on a stretcher
and the truck in the distance
burst into a blaze.

EVERY BREATH, A PRAYER

(San Quintin, Baja California 1983)

Fernando, *el mixteco*,
climbs the red dirt of baja hills
along rain-drenched paths
and wades through a field of waist-high grass.
He stops at a clearing where a rainbow
of piled stones,
colored sticks, and flowers
shares communion with the ground
of the living
to the ground of the dead.

Dozens of baby graves fill the hillside:
little ones in shoebox-size coffins
adorned with painted rock, sea shells,
and wooden crosses, sprinkled with dry leaves.
They are buried near the tomato plants
where some 80,000
Mixteco Indians are seasonally
enslaved.

Fernando, *el mixteco,*
leaves his plastic and carton shack
and passes an old irrigation pump
where his 3-year-old boy
was crushed in the mesh of steel gears
on a Sunday of play.

Fernando crisscrosses
the sutured earth
alongside the fires that light
the glazed faces of mothers

squatting with diseased children
in the heart of dust.

He steps across a rotting plank
used as a bridge over a stream
as a woman leans over
pushing rags wet against the rocks
and another nearby
pressing a crusted nipple
to the mouth of a baby;
its every breath, a prayer.

Fernando, *el mixteco,*
then eyes the north
where a wind comes and ruffles
his thick hair
as he declares death to death,
his eyes dark with
the hollow of unborn days.

Fernando's body becomes the sides
of a native dirt-brick house,
his hair turns into a tarred-paper
and branched roof;
an arm becomes a child becomes home.

THIS TREE, THIS POEM

(to Noni)

This tree, this poem,
is about life,
abundance in green
where forests are fuel,
breathing for the world.
A tree is like a woman,
the bark of skin
blemished by birth.
Or it could be a boy,
branches swaying free;
a martyr of hours
coming home on the wings of a storm.
Sometimes I see a tree
and I see a daughter
seeking the fatherhood of oaks.

This tree, this poem,
stands alone in a blanket of green
and takes in its lust of air
filling the gap from oceans
to this clay in the rain called man.
We dance around trees,
dance for the fall of leaves,
dance, until wind-swept and scattered
we descend like fine dew,
or tears, tracing lines
on a trunk's stitched face.

We need trees like we need
the rail ties that carry us,
the fences between us—

the paper poems are scribbled on.
We need trees to sing
a silent sonata of bloom.

This tree, this poem,
is smothering in the city's crush.
It rises through cement cracks
like the earth invading,
reminding,
protesting,
and demands the sky.

But the skull of dark days
is also carved on the bark;
branches screaming
with the strange fruit
of swaying bodies.

A tree is a friend,
a child's playroom,
or a gallows.
We make of trees
what we make of ourselves.

THEN COMES A DAY

The Resurrection Cemetery is an oasis of green,
encircled by the rising structures of the Edison
Utility Company and new roads interwoven through
the felled homes that once flowered with families.

The hills are sprinkled with the remains
of wood-frame shacks, splinters of the old
neighborhood that gentrification, progress,
and new "immigrants," this time with money,
have discolored.

It has been twenty years since I roamed these
earthen streets. Coming back, I am as new, alien,
except in that old cemetery where many of my
friends are buried: Dead by drugs, by gangs,
by police, by suicide, car crashes, and diseases
science conquered long ago.

In the end, what does it matter how they died!
The heart is only a beating thing. They left,
unconscious of the stars shimmering without them.
Still their time in the world echoes as secrets
in the rhythm of night. The earth may have their
fingers, but not what they touched: The contours
of skin beneath folds of an ocean's wave, the laminated
sweat on a brow—the sinew of an open-wound dream.

Every death was new life, becoming like the pacing
in a waking sleep that pounds into the realm
of impelling memory. So many funerals. So many dark
cruises through these curbless paths; revenge,
as thick as mud, in the windless air. All that's left
of that time are the headstones under sodden skies;

the bleeding of wombs as revolution is birthed
through an open-mouth scream. Coming back,
the quiet becomes relentless in the repose.

I have carried the obligation to these names.
I have honored their voices
still reverberating through me.
Even now, as the fight flourishes through
the burden of days, the rage has only
subsided to deeper seas.

Justice is the long, crevice-filled road
I've been stranded on all this time,
trying to reach a destination that climbs
uneasy over the horizon. I owe it to them
to stay. I owe it to them to await the daybreak
tearing out of the long night in the battlements.

And I can see the first light coming into view.
And I can hear their pleas through the hush.
And I remember: Twenty years come
that don't make a day,
then comes a day
that makes up
for twenty years.

CURBSTONE PRESS, INC.

is a non-profit publishing house dedicated to literature that reflects a commitment to social change, with an emphasis on contemporary writing from Latino, Latin American and Vietnamese cultures. Curbstone presents writers who give voice to the unheard in a language that goes beyond denunciation to celebrate, honor and teach. Curbstone builds bridges between its writers and the public – from inner-city to rural areas, colleges to community centers, children to adults. Curbstone seeks out the highest aesthetic expression of the dedication to human rights and intercultural understanding: poetry, testimonies, novels, stories, and children's books.

This mission requires more than just producing books. It requires ensuring that as many people as possible learn about these books and read them. To achieve this, a large portion of Curbstone's schedule is dedicated to arranging tours and programs for its authors, working with public school and university teachers to enrich curricula, reaching out to underserved audiences by donating books and conducting readings and community programs, and promoting discussion in the media. It is only through these combined efforts that literature can truly make a difference.

Curbstone Press, like all non-profit presses, depends on the support of individuals, foundations, and government agencies to bring you, the reader, works of literary merit and social significance which might not find a place in profit-driven publishing channels, and to bring the authors and their books into communities across the country. Our sincere thanks to the many individuals, foundations, and government agencies who support this endeavor: J. Walton Bissell Foundation, Connecticut Commission on the Arts, Connecticut Humanities Council, Fisher Foundation, Greater Hartford Arts Council, Hartford Courant Foundation, J. M. Kaplan Fund, Eric Mathieu King Fund, John D. and Catherine T. MacArthur Foundation, National Endowment for the Arts, Open Society Institute, and the Woodrow Wilson National Fellowship Foundation.

Please help to support Curbstone's efforts to present the diverse voices and views that make our culture richer. Tax-deductible donations can be made by check or credit card to:
Curbstone Press, 321 Jackson Street, Willimantic, CT 06226
phone: (860) 423-5110   fax: (860) 423-9242
www.curbstone.org

IF YOU WOULD LIKE TO BE A MAJOR SPONSOR OF A CURBSTONE BOOK, PLEASE CONTACT US.